T0105331

6,0
5,6
5,0
4,6
4,0
3,1
3,0
2,6
WHO INVENTED CROWD FUNDING?
AFRAID OF SUSPECTS
FIVE MUSICIANS . ONE INTERNET . NO LABEL .

MARILLION SOUNDS THAT CAN'T BE MADE

marillion brave

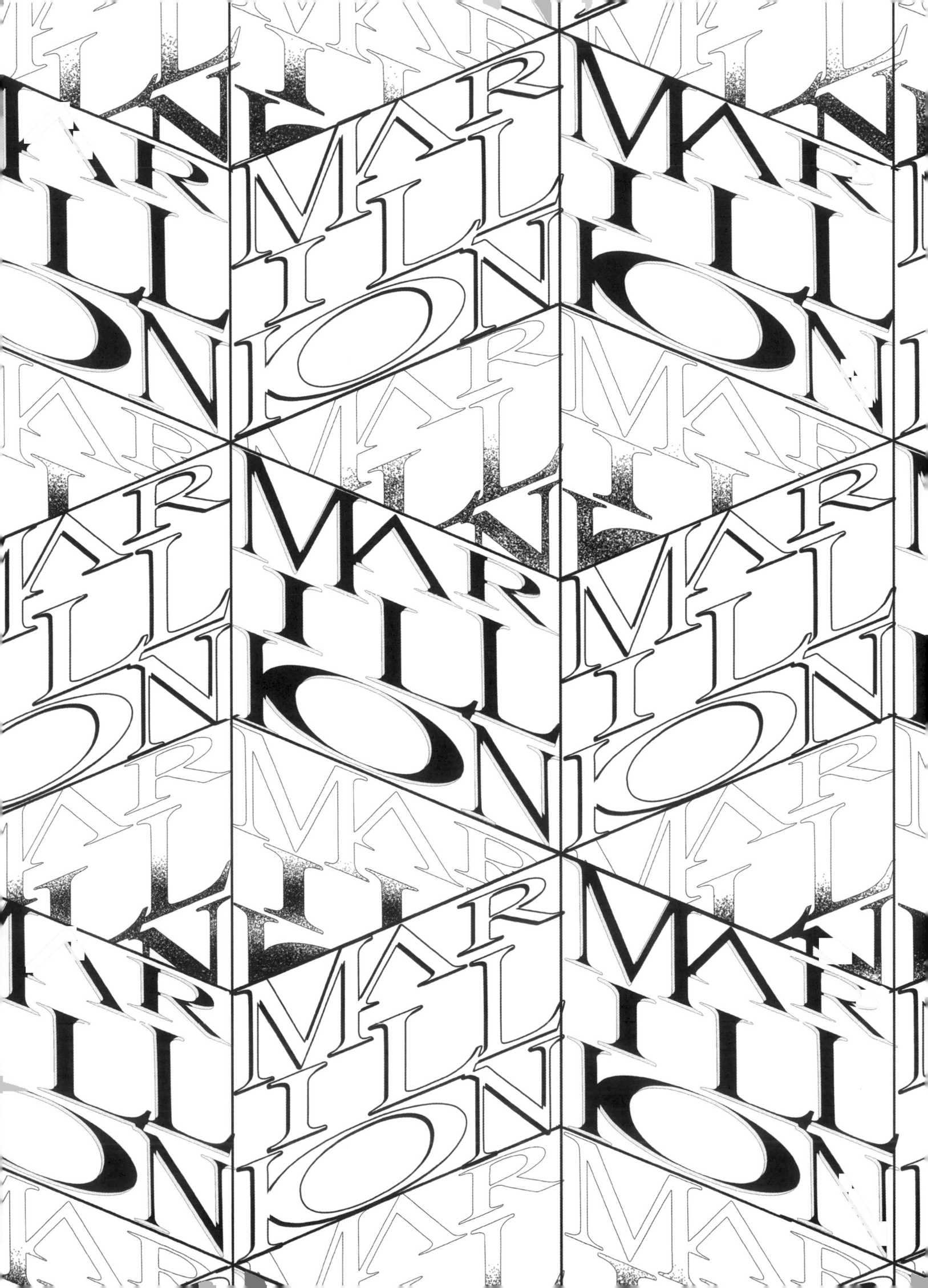
MARMILNION

MARILLION

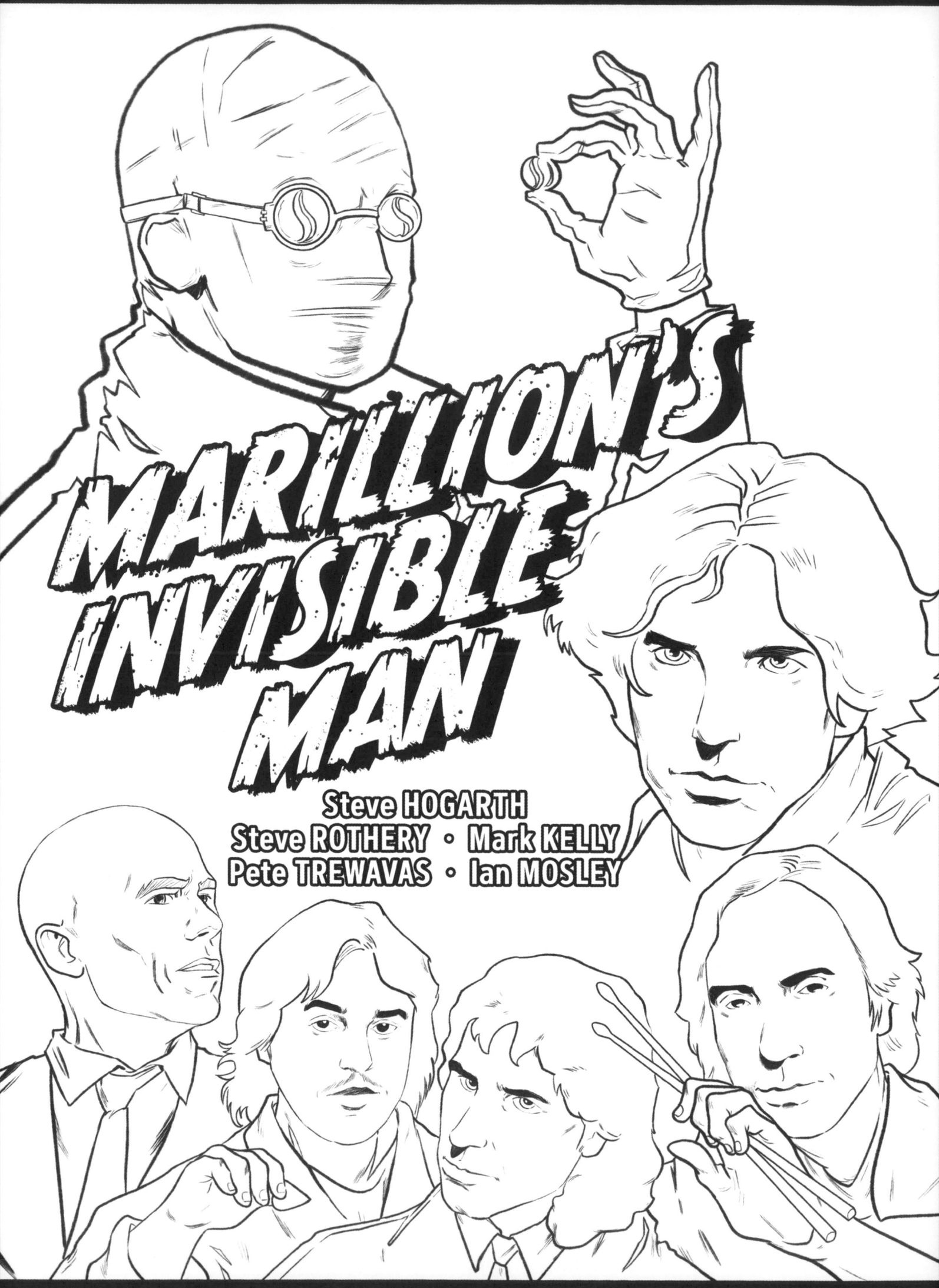
MARILLION'S
INVISIBLE
MAN
Steve HOGARTH
Steve ROTHERY • Mark KELLY
Pete TREWAVAS • Ian MOSLEY

Visit
BERLIN
...just listen
to track #6
of Seasons End.

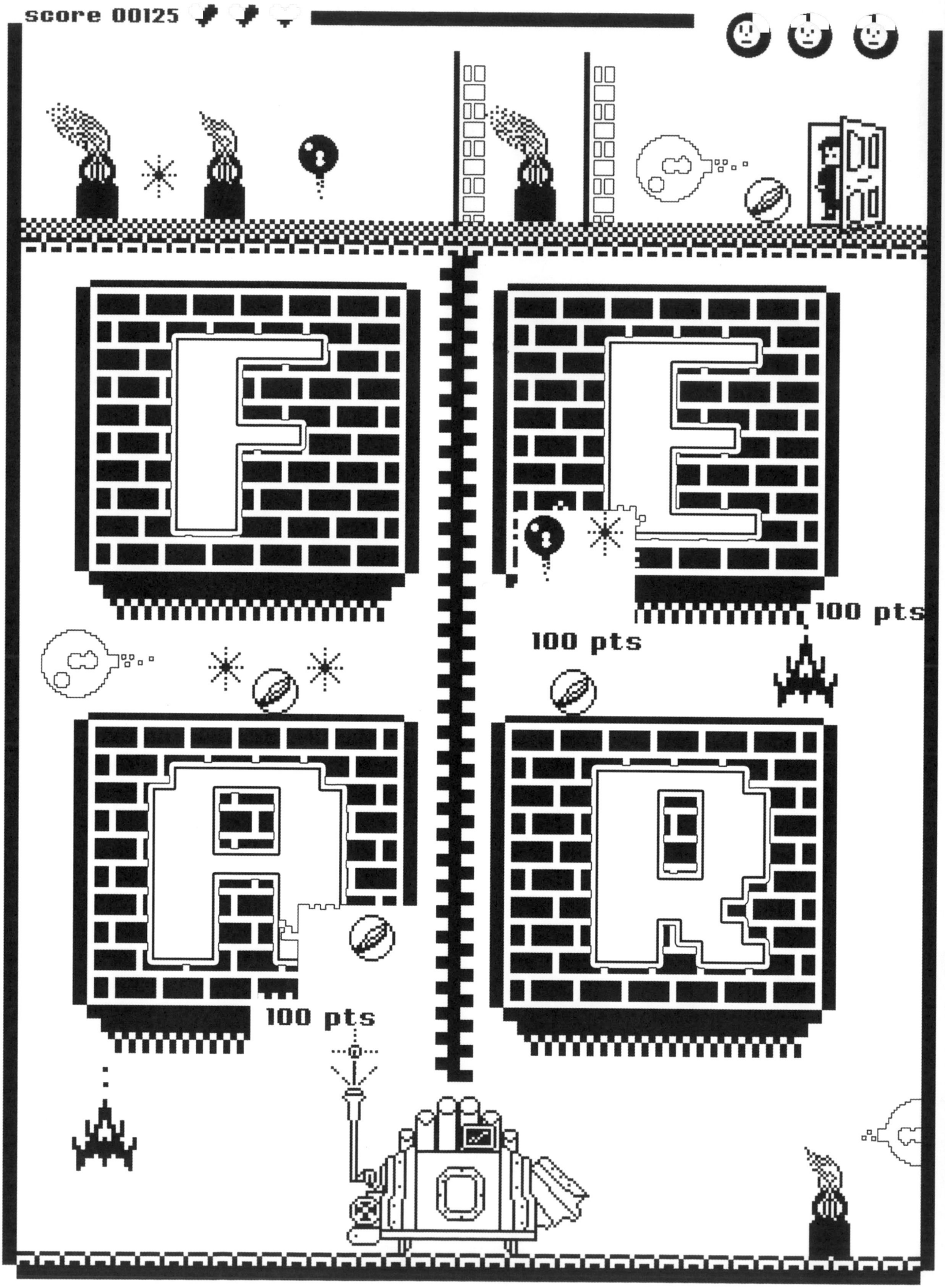
score 00125
100 pts
100 pts
100 pts

M·A·R·I·L·L·I·O·N
COUCH CONVENTION

marillion
colours and sound

Afraid of sunlight?
PROGGERTONE

HA HA HA

HOMEMADE GAZPACHO
MARILLION

HARRY HOUDINI
LIVE AT THE
COLISEUM

Be Brave
X
100
NIGHTS
FEAR

CHANGE

NOLIRIOLIMIN

Kellyggs
SPECIAL H
CEREAL
MADE WITH
100%
ORGANIC
RADIATION!
NOW WITH HIDDEN MARBLES IN EVERY BOX!
10G
IANDINE
120G
STEVEIUM
40G
PETETASSIUM

MARILLION

PSYCHIATRIC
HELP 5p.
THE MANAGER
IS IN

FEAR
MIKE
HUNTER

MARILLION
COMICS
ISSUE #1989
Marillion
COMICS

MARILLION
HOLIDAYS IN EDEN

END HERE
MARIGOLD
START HERE

END
START
MARILLION SOUNDS THAT CAN´T BE MADE

HOW ABOUT IT, MR. KIMMEL?

MARILLION

Ho

Ed

No

Br

Gr

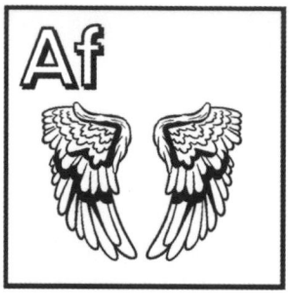
Af

Af²

Be

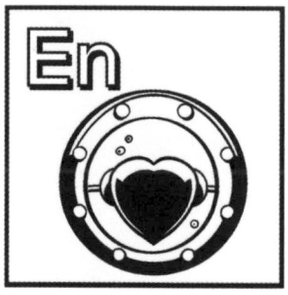
En

Ch

Ra

Po

Cm

Ak UK

Aw

El

Fa

In

Jn

Mr
CHANGE

Ra

Sm

Pu

Fe
F

Bb

Sz

Sw

Sw Ln

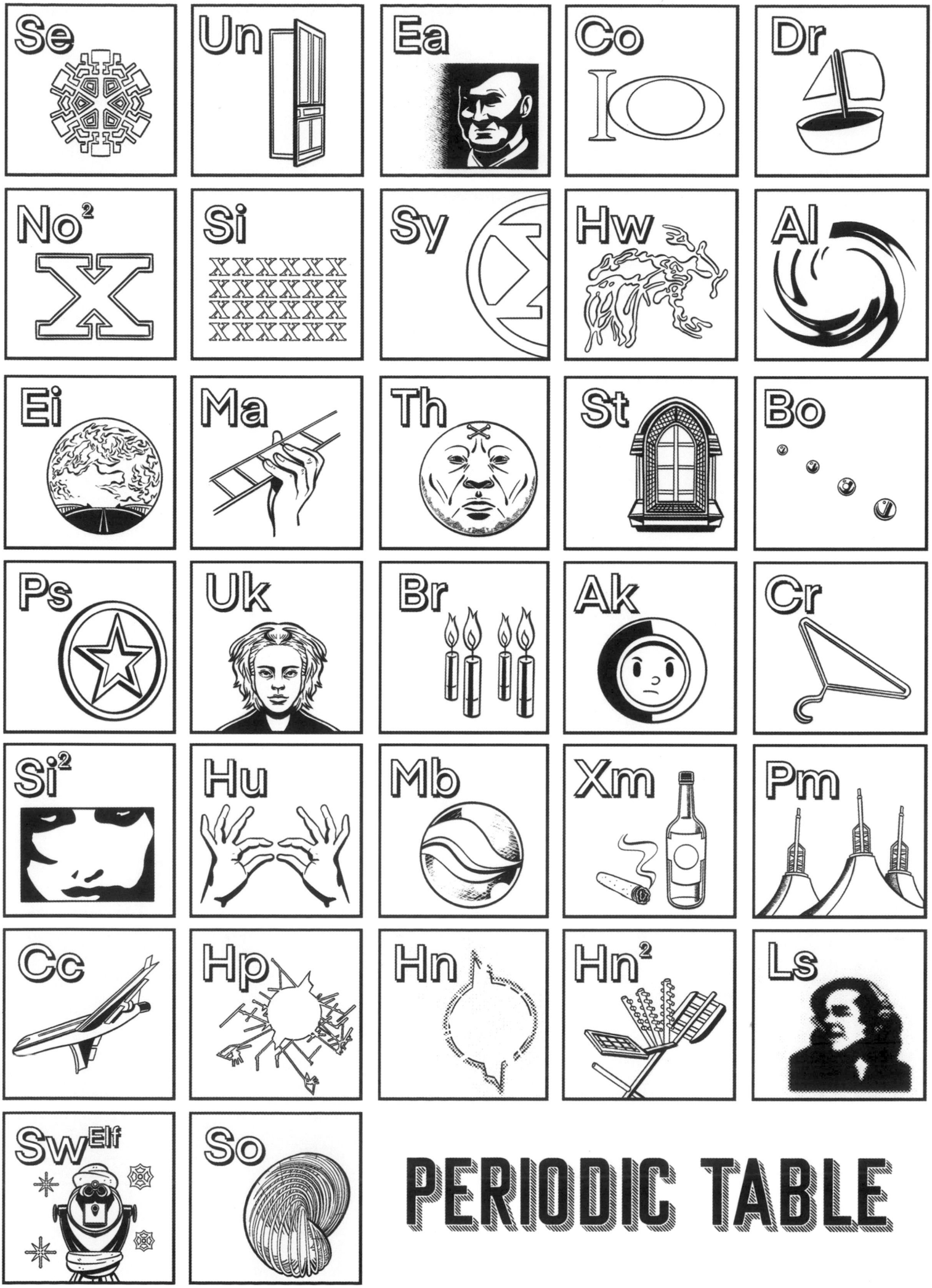

PERIODIC TABLE

MAN
OF A
1000
FACES

007
JOHN BARRY
CAMEL
The Snow Goose

MARILLION
COFFEE DAYS IN EDEN

WAITING TO HAPPEN
MARILLION COFFEE

LIVE IN CARACAS

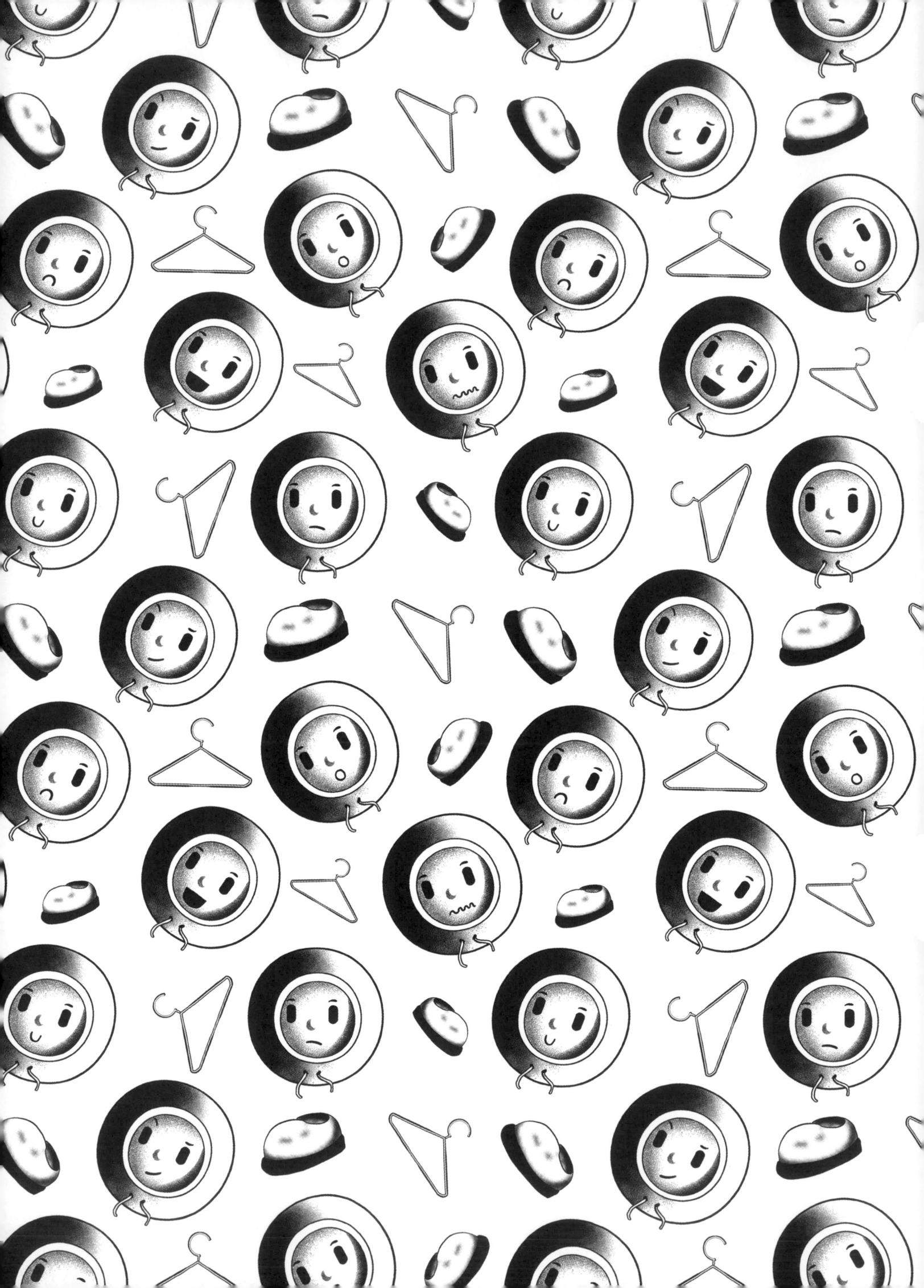

MARILLION

MARILLION
Seasons End

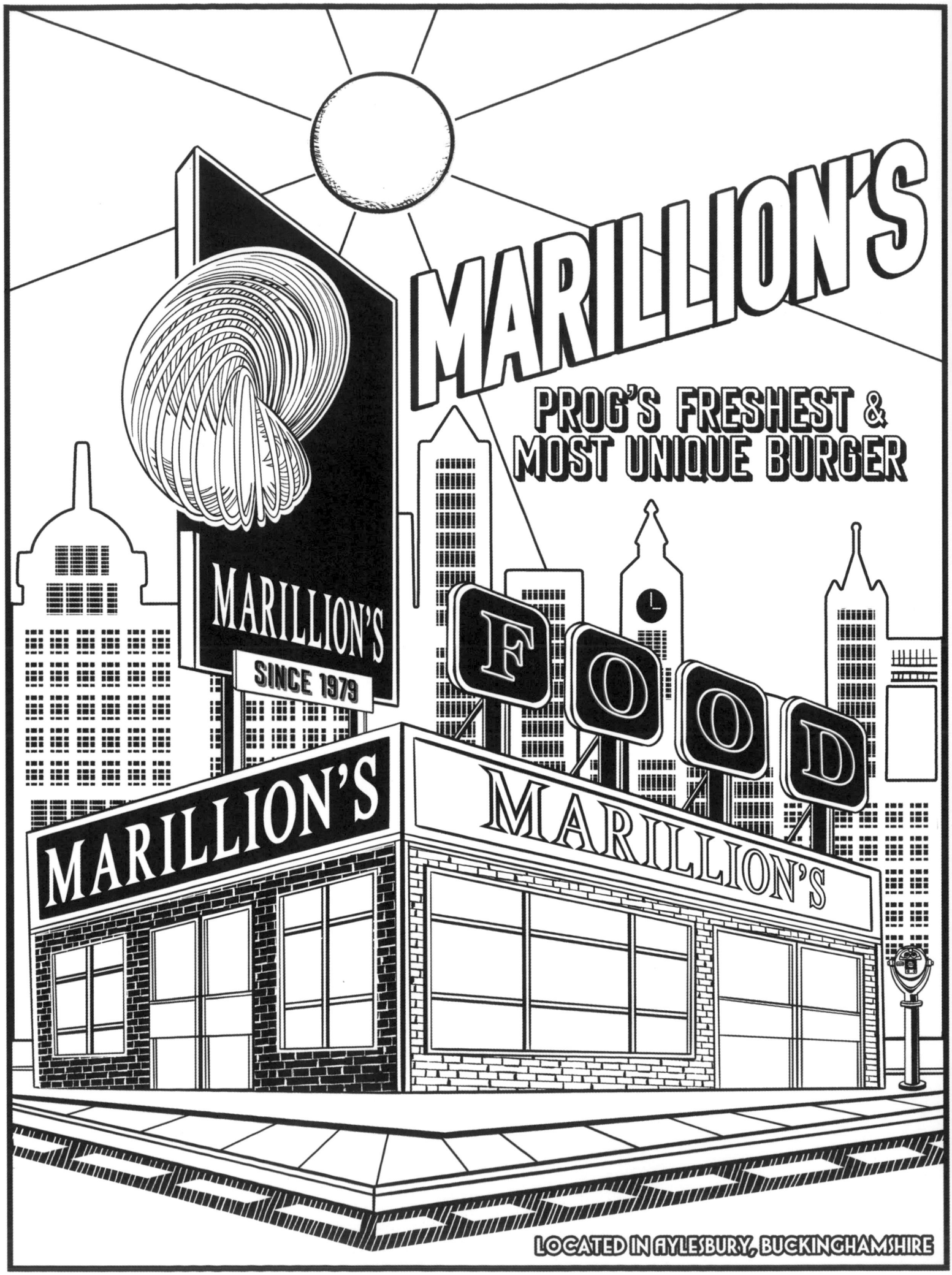
MARILLION'S
PROG'S FRESHEST &
MOST UNIQUE BURGER
MARILLION'S
SINCE 1979
FOOD
MARILLION'S
MARILLION'S
LOCATED IN AYLESBURY, BUCKINGHAMSHIRE

MARILLION'S
MENU
BEAUTIFUL BURGER
COVER MY EGGS
IAN MUESLY
BREAKFAST
BRAVE TACOS
DRY LAMB
GAZPACHO
DRINKS
Coca-Kelly
COCA-KELLY
ROTHEBEER
TEAWAVAS

BRITISH
DRUM CO.
BRITISH
DRUM CO.

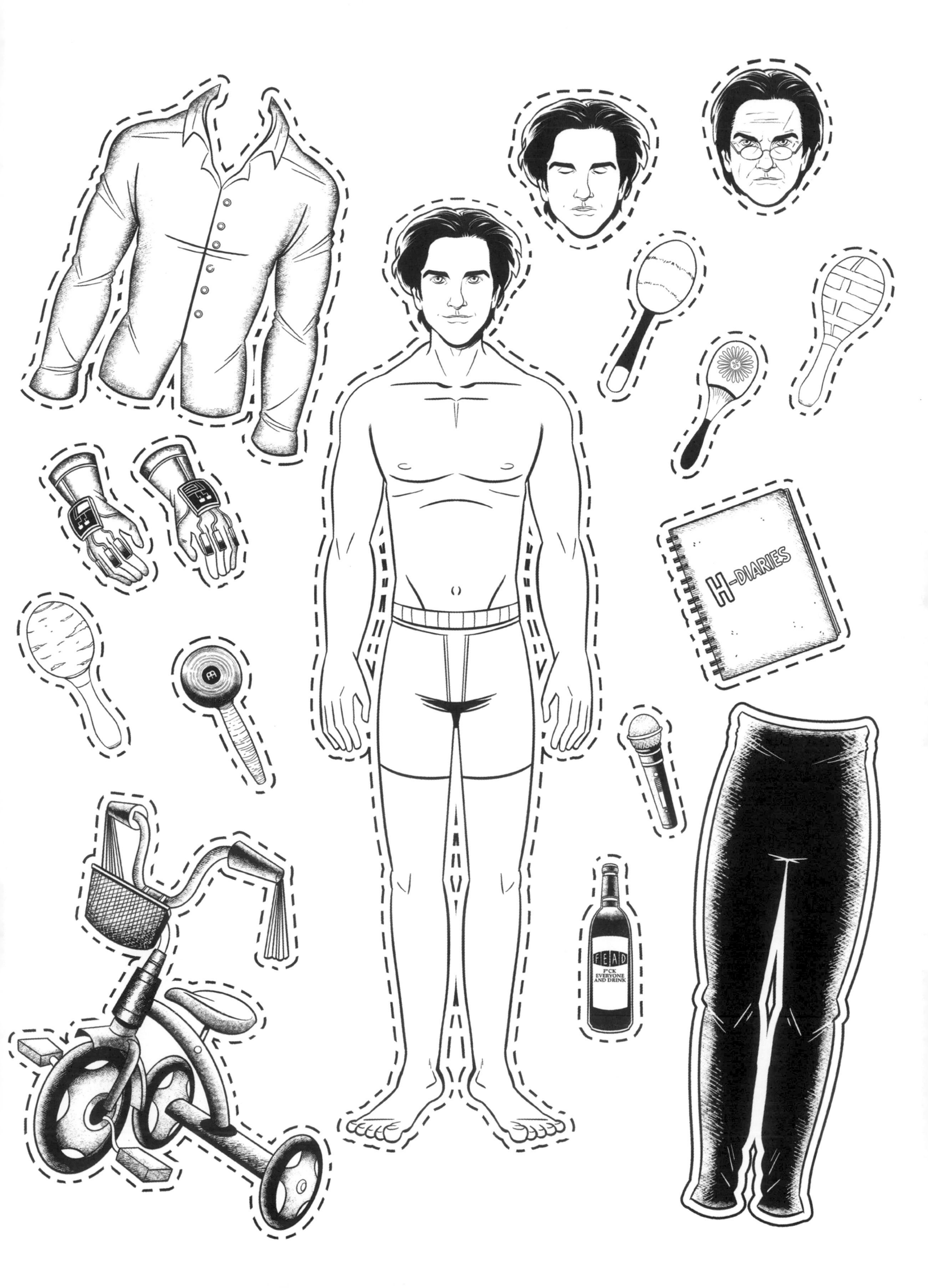
H-DIARIES
FEAD
F*CK
EVERYONE
AND DRINK

STUCK IN DRYLAND?
ERNATIONALLY RECORDED
1991
100
NIGHTS
EXTRA PROG
HOOK END MANOR, OXFORDSHIRE

HOGARTH.
HAPPY CHRISTMAS

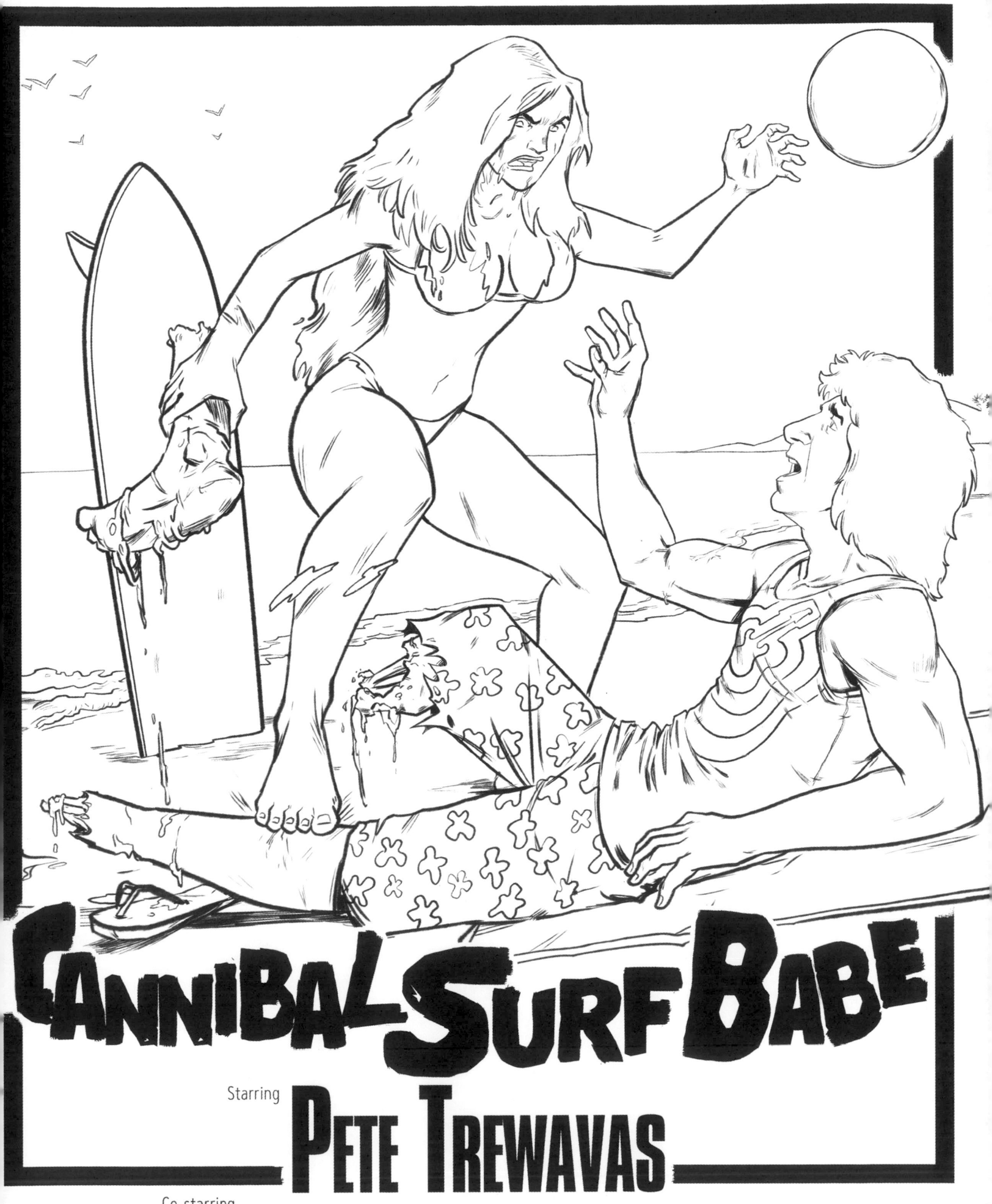
CANNIBAL SURF BABE
Starring
PETE TREWAVAS
Co-starring
LUCY JORDACHE · IAN MOSLEY · LADY NINA · MR. H
Written by: MARK KELLY · Directed by: GADGET MAN · Produced by: RACKET BROTHERS PICTURES

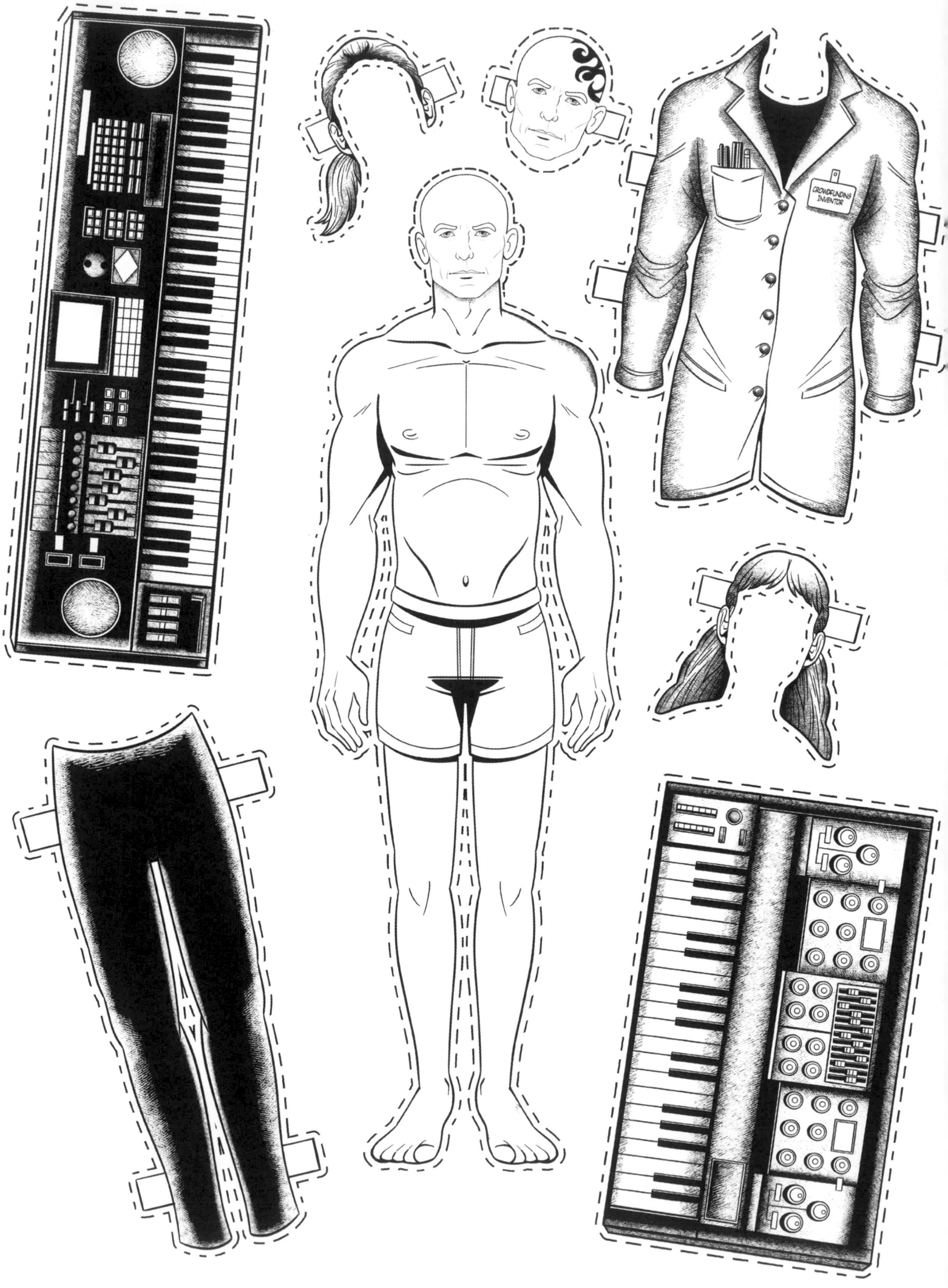
CROWDFUNDING
INVENTOR

MARILLION
THE UNINVITED GUEST 2600
9 COSMIC GAMES
• FROGS AND FEAR
• REAL SPORTS MARBLES 2600
• SUPER ANORAKNOPHOBIA
• SEASONS END QUEST 2600
• THE GREAT ESCAPE II
• RADIATION REVENGE
+ THREE BONUS GAMES

THE ~~FOUR~~ FIVE
MARILLION
BROTHERS

WELCOME
TO COSTA DEL
SLOUGH

Marillion
NEVERLAND

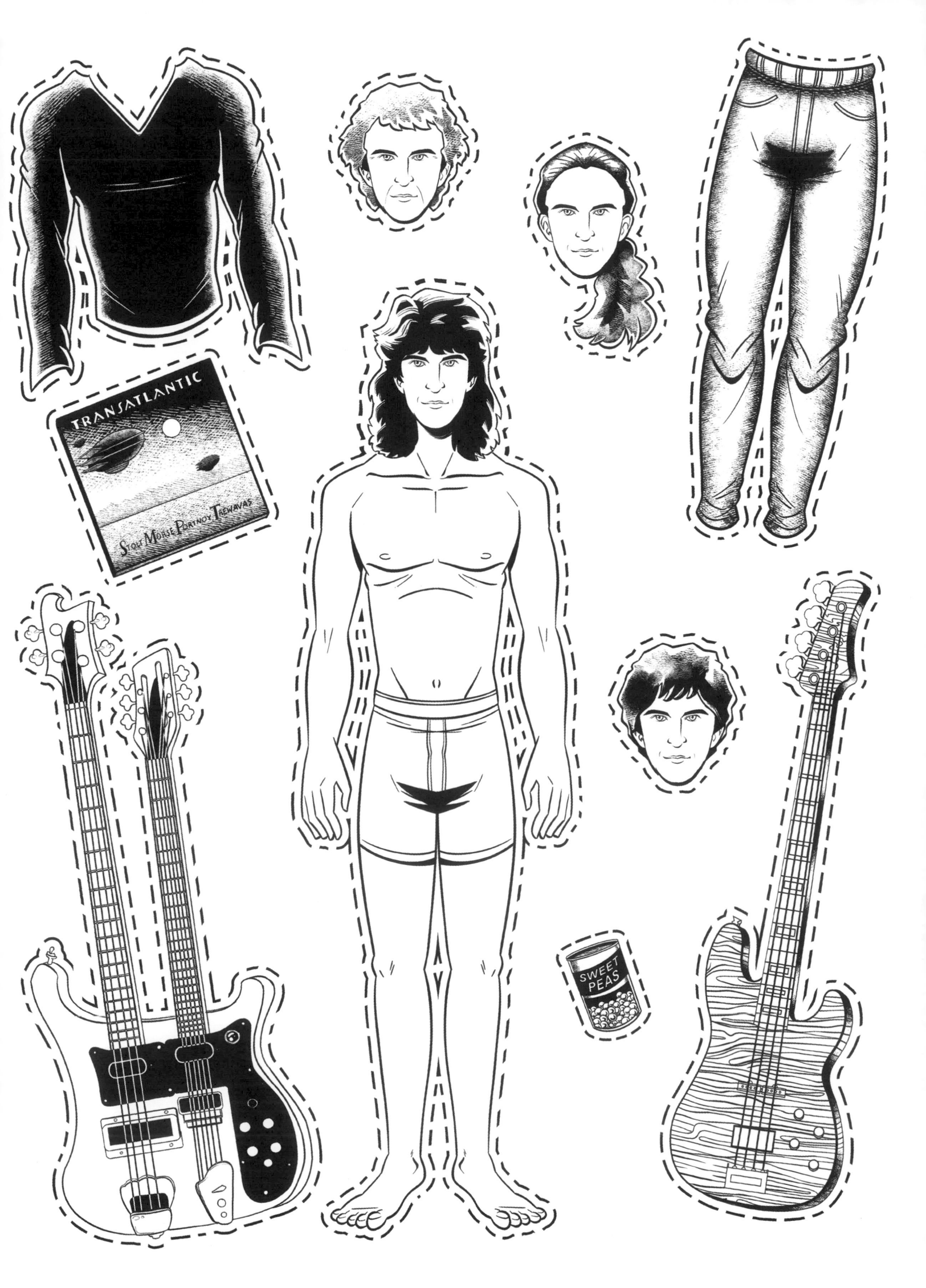
TRANSATLANTIC
STOLT MORSE PORTNOY TREWAVAS
SWEET PEAS

MARILLION
A MONSTROUSLY FESTIVE(AL) CHRISTMAS
CHRISTMAS 2015

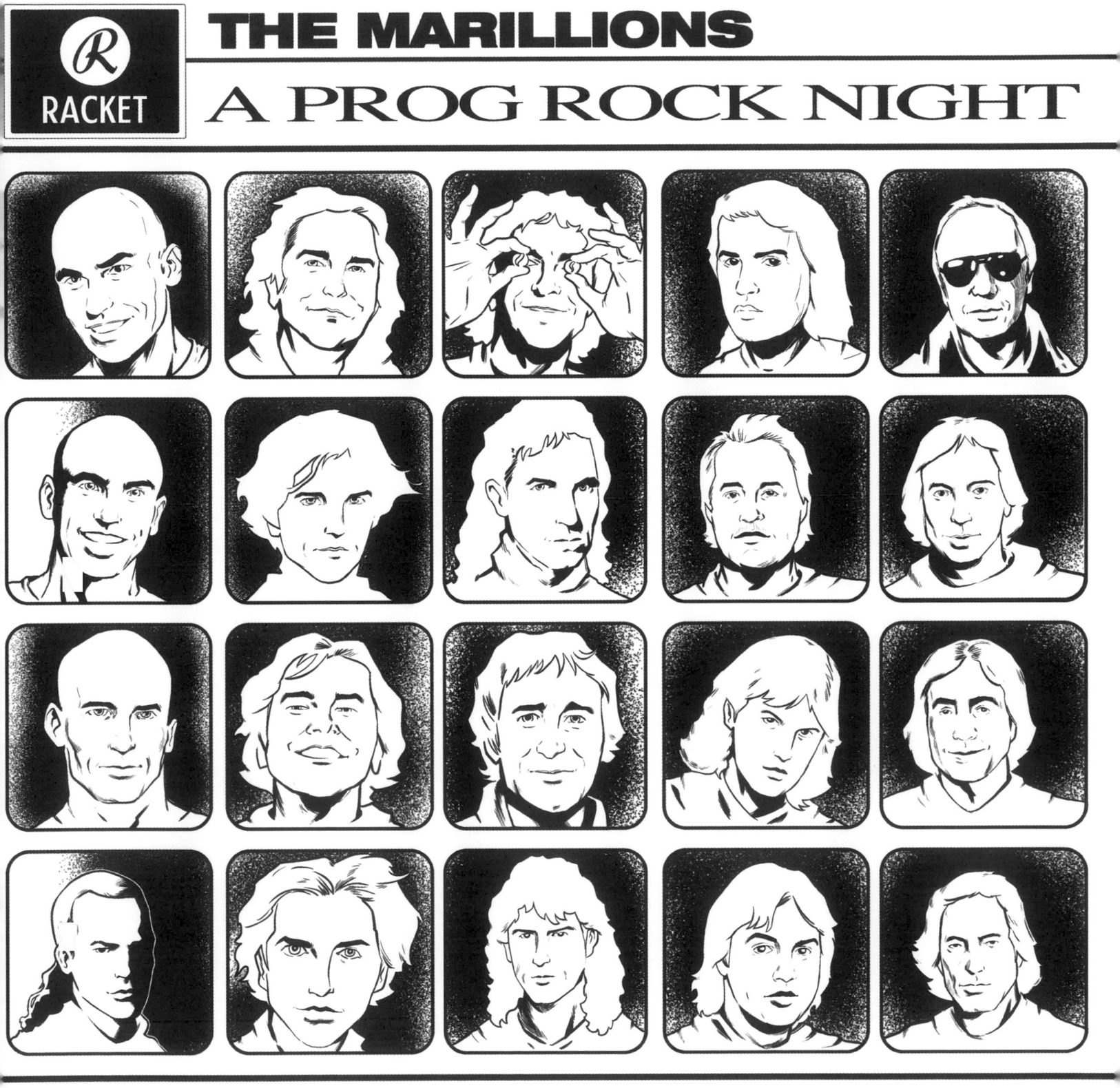
R
RACKET
THE MARILLIONS
A PROG ROCK NIGHT

3 MINUTE BOY

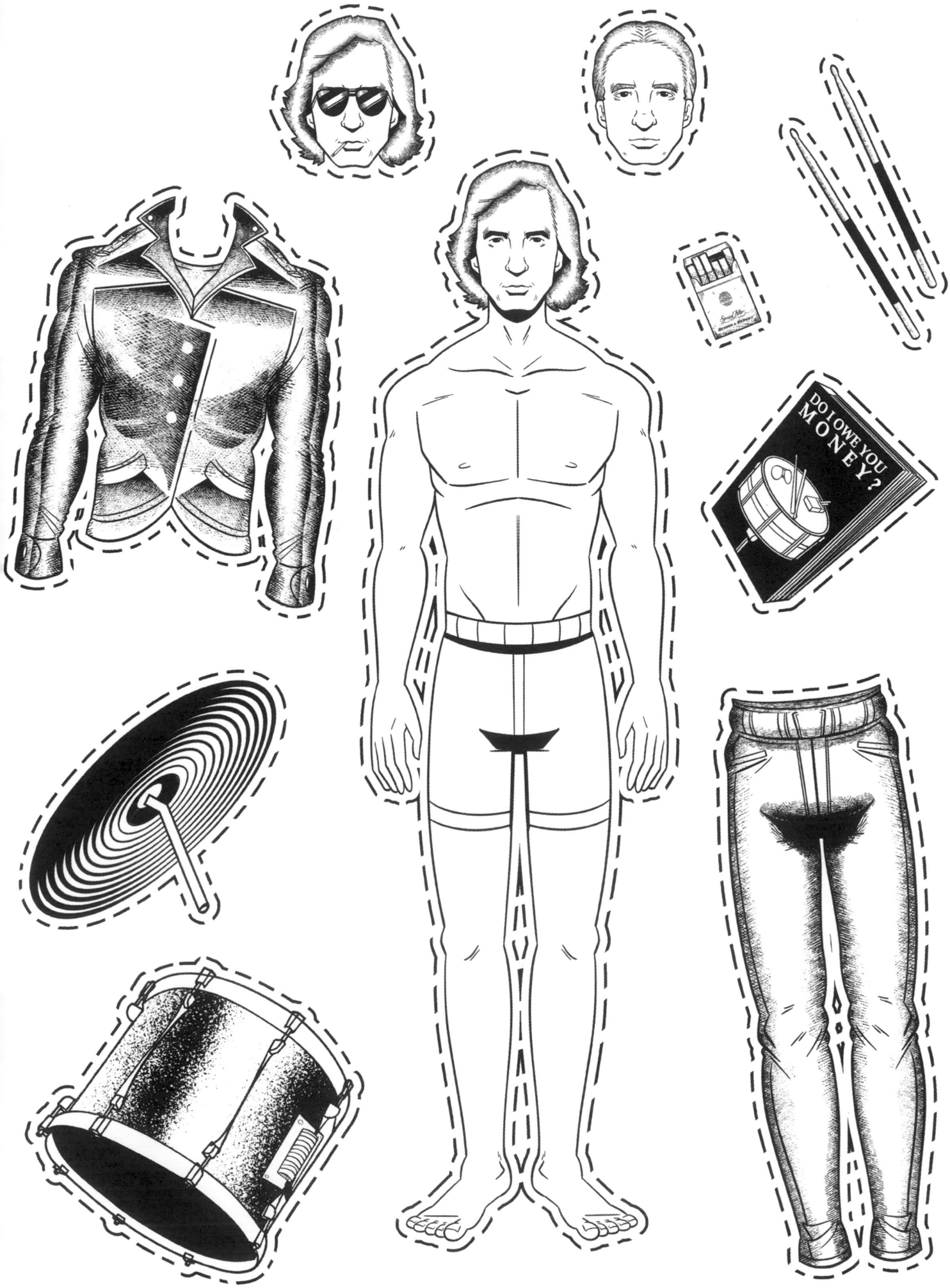
DO I OWE YOU
MONEY?

MA
RI
LLI
ON!

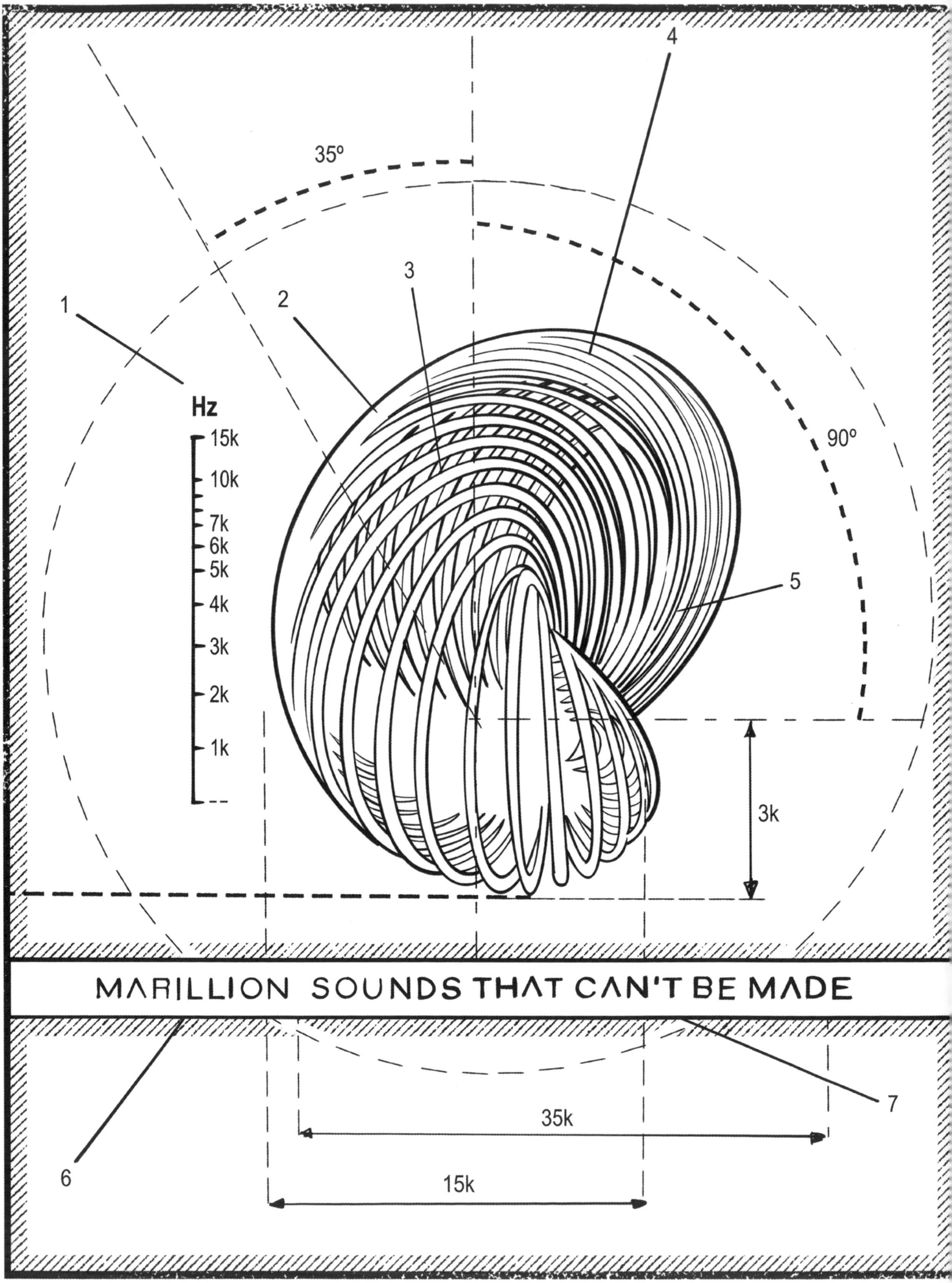
4
35°
3
2
1
Hz
15k
10k
7k
6k
5k
4k
3k
2k
1k
90°
5
3k
MARILLION SOUNDS THAT CAN'T BE MADE
7
35k
6
15k

MARILLION